Text Copyright © Katrina Streza 2012
Illustration Copyright © Brenda Ponnay 2012

All Rights Reserved. No portion of this book may be reproduced without express permission from the publisher.
First Edition
ISBN-13: 9781623954741
Published in the United States by Xist Publishing
www.xistpublishing.com
PO Box 61593 Irvine, CA 92602

xist Publishing

My Good Dog

By Katrina Streza
illustrated by Brenda Ponnay

My dog is a good dog.

My dog can sit.

My dog can sit on my foot.

My dog cannot sit on my face.

My dog can bark.

My dog can bark at the moon.

My dog cannot bark on the moon.

My dog can jump.

My dog can jump over a rock.

My dog cannot jump over my house.

My dog can run.

My dog can run fast.

My dog cannot run as fast as a car.

My dog can play.

My dog can play with me.

My dog cannot play with my fish.

My dog can see.

My dog can see the little birds fly.

My dog cannot fly with the little birds.

My dog can eat.

My dog can eat dog food.

My dog cannot eat my food.

My dog can sleep.

My dog can sleep on a bed.

Snzzzssss
snnzzzzsss

My dog cannot sleep on my bed.

My dog is a good dog.

Want to read more about the dog?

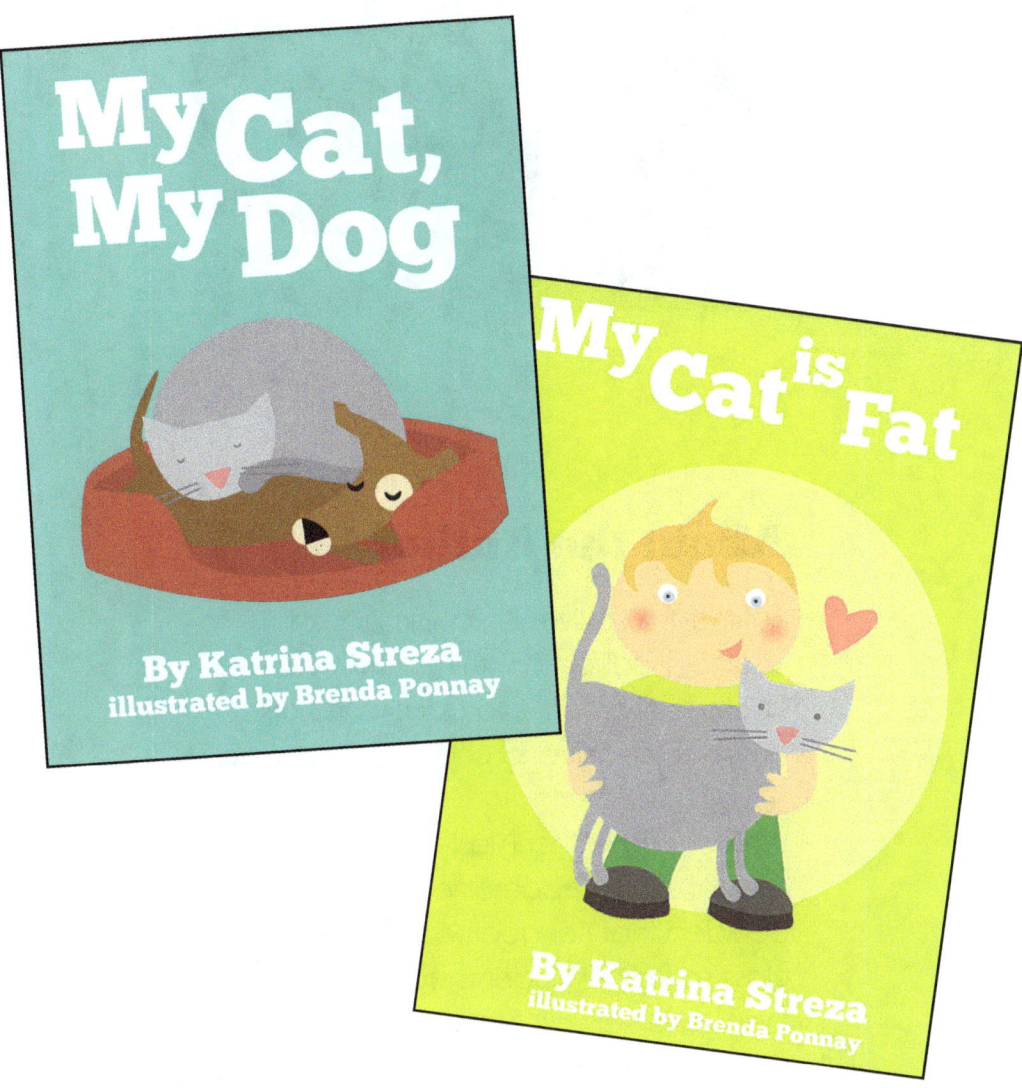

Don't Miss the Other Books!

About the Author

Katrina Streza lives on a small ranch in Southern California with her family, twelve chickens, two cats, two dogs, one horse, one baby goat and one very noisy dove.

While receiving her Master's Degree in Education at Pepperdine University, Katrina decided that her goal was to make class so fun her students wouldn't realize they were learning. She's applied that philosophy while teaching and tutoring kids from kindergarten to college.

About the Illustrator

Brenda Ponnay is the author and illustrator of several children's books including the Time for Bunny series and Secret Agent Josephine series. She lives in Southern California with her daughter, Bug* who inspires her daily.

You can read all about their crazy adventures on her personal blog: www.secret-agent-josephine.com

*Not her real name.

www.ingramcontent.com/pod-product-compliance
Lightning Source LLC
LaVergne TN
LVHW021600070426
835507LV00014B/1884